Where do Siths do all their shopping?

At the Darth Mall.

Why did Yoda always carry a pencil?

Because he had a point to make, he did.

Why did Chewbacca get a GPS?

Because even Wookiees can get hairy in traffic.

Why did Yoda never hold in his farts?

Because the Force must flow.

Why was Darth Vader so angry in math class?

Because he found your lack of division disturbing.

Why did Princess Leia refuse to play hide and seek?

Because she didn’t want to be Solo.

Why did Obi-Wan start a gardening business?

Because he had the best mulch in the galaxy.

Why did R2-D2 always win arguments?

Because his beeps were always so logical and clear.

Why did Yoda fail as a stand-up comedian?

Because his jokes felt forced.

Why did Vader avoid art class?

Because he couldn't draw breath.

Why did the Millennium Falcon smell like a wet dog?

Because Chewie was always in the cockpit.

What do you call a nervous Jedi?

Panickin' Skywalker.

Why did Boba Fett never become a comedian?

Because his jokes always went over people's heads.

Why did Darth Vader hate selfies?

Because he couldn't stand seeing himself unmasked.

Why did Yoda refuse credit cards?

Because cash only, he does.

What is Luke's best dance move?

The Skywalk.

What is Grogu's favorite dessert?

Force-fed ice cream!

Why was Han Solo angry with his GPS?

Because it told him he couldn't do
the Kessel Run in 12 parsecs.

What did Obi-Wan Kenobi say after he farted?

"I felt a disturbance in the Force."

Why did Boba Fett start using sunscreen?

Because Tatooine is tough on Mandalorian armor.

Why did Grogu get kicked out of daycare?

Because he used the Force to steal cookies.

What is Mando's favorite song to sing at karaoke nights?

"This is the Way" by the Mandalorians.

Why did the TIE Fighter get relegated?

Because it had too many draws.

Why did the Star Destroyer go to therapy?

Because it had control issues.

Why did the droids open a bakery?

Because they wanted to make R2-Dough2.

Why was the Death Star bad at stand-up comedy?

Because its jokes kept bombing.

Why did C-3PO open a dance studio?

Because he had great moves for metallic grooves.

Why did Chewbacca refuse to text?

Because typing is hard with paws.

Why did Yoda avoid smartphones?

Because fear of attachment, he had.

Why did R2-D2 write a blog?

Because he had lots of bytes.

Why did the Ewoks open a resort?

Because they wanted a tree-mendous business.

Why did Endor love hide-and-seek?

Because it was full of hiding spots.

Why did Padmé call her fart "The Phantom Menace"?

Because you never see it coming.

Why was the Death Star a terrible tourist spot?

Because it had zero atmosphere.

Why did Vader cross the road?

To get to the dark side.

Why did Yoda visit Starbucks?

For a frappuccino, he wanted.

Why did Chewbacca open a Wookie hair salon?

Because business was hairy good.

Why did R2-D2 love karaoke?

Because he could hit all the high beeps.

Why was everyone scared to fight R2-D2?

Because he had too many loose screws.

What's Baby Yoda's favorite search engine?

Grogoogle.

Why did the Sith hate comedians?

Because laughter is the light side.

Why did the Stormtrooper buy an iPhone?

Because he couldn't find the droid he was looking for.

Why did Vader love coffee?

Because he craved the dark roast.

Why did Yoda never get lost?

Because there is no try, only GPS.

Why did Anakin hate bean burritos?

Because they awakened the Dark Side in him.

What do you call a Jedi who loves to nap?

Yawn Solo!

Why was R2-D2 bad at basketball?

He kept short-circuiting on the dunk!

How does Yoda stay in shape?

He does Jedi-lates every morning!

Why did the Ewok start a band?

Because he wanted to rock the Endor!

What's Jabba the Hutt's favorite snack?

Hoth dogs!

Why was the Death Star so unpopular?

It kept blowing up the party!

How does Yoda deal with constipation?

He uses the Force.

Why was the Millennium Falcon so messy?

Han never took out the trash compactor!

Why didn't C-3PO mind Chewbacca's awful farts?

Because his sensors couldn't process the smell.

Why did Count Dooku start a fencing club?

Because “saber etiquette” is a lost art.

Why did Darth Sidious never lose a debate?

Because every argument ended with "Good… GOOD."

Why did Boba Fett install surround sound in his ship?

Because bounty hunting needs more bass.

Why did Luke take his lightsaber to a dance?

Because he wanted to cut the rug.

Why did Leia bring extra batteries?

Because her hair buns were wired for sound.

Why did Chewbacca buy a hairdryer?

Because hyperspace winds make bad hair days worse.

What was the first thing Yoda said on his podcast?

"Share wisdom, I must."

Why did Vader avoid buffets?

Because he found their lack of structure disturbing.

Why do Stormtroopers make bad basketball players?

Because they can't hit anything.

Why did the clone army start a choir?

Because they were always in perfect harmony.

Why did BB-8 join the dance floor?

Because he liked rolling with the beat.

Why did Yoda never argue online?

Because “trolls, a path to the dark side they are.”

Why did Darth Vader's helmet fog up?

Because even the dark side can't prevent a fart.

Why did C-3PO never play poker?

Because he always gave off nervous signals.

Why did a clone ask for a raise?

Because he felt like just another number.

Why did Chewie stop playing charades with Han?

Because “RAWRRRGH” was too easy to guess.

Why did Kylo Ren never tell jokes?

Because he always goes too dark.

Why did R2-D2 go to the dentist?

To fix his Bluetooth.

What's a Jedi's favorite dessert?

Obi-Wan Cannoli.

What's a Wookiee's favorite instrument?

The hair-monium.

What do you call five Siths piled on top of a lightsaber?

A Sith-kabob.

Why did Darth Vader go to the mall?

To find the dark side of the food court.

Why did the Millennium Falcon break up with the X-Wing?

Because it needed some space.

What did Luke say to the waiter?

"May the forks be with you."

What's Yoda's favorite exercise?

Do-or-do-not squats.

What did one lightsaber say when it proposed to the other lightsaber?

"You light up my world."

What's Vader's favorite type of ice cream?

Dark chocolate chip.

Why did Yoda call his fart "the dark side"?

Because once it's unleashed, all hope fades.

Why did Luke Skywalker fail art class?

Because he kept drawing a blank saber.

Why did Grogu eat his homework?

Because the Force was hungry.

What's Vader's favorite type of music?

Heavy breathing metal.

What's Darth Maul's favorite workout?

Sith ups!

What's Jabba's favorite snack?

Hoth fudge sundaes!

Why did the Death Star succeed as a hotel?

Because it had so many explosive reviews!

What's Chewbacca's favorite instrument?

The Wookiee-lele!

Why did Chewbacca never win poker?

Because he always growled when bluffing.

Why did Grogu try to eat Leia's hair?

He thought it was cinnamon buns.

What's Chewbacca's breakfast restaurant called?

Wookie Waffles.

Why did BB-8 hate playing soccer?

Because everyone tried to kick him in the net.

Why did R2-D2 love movie night?

Because he had built-in projectors.

What do you call a Sith with a sweet tooth?

Darth Chocolate.

Why did Kylo Ren hate yoga?

Because he can’t balance the dark side.

Why did C-3PO hate the dentist?

Because the dentist kept asking him to open his mouth.

Why did Chewie love winter holidays?

Because no one can out-fur him in ugly sweaters.

Why did the Stormtroopers fail photography class?

Because they kept missing the shots.

What did Darth Vader say after Luke's fart exploded the Death Star.

"The Force is strong with this one."

Printed in Dunstable, United Kingdom

71205144R00057